TO SEE A KING

TO SEE A KING

PROPHETESS NEKESHIA GIBSON
Sherita Gayden

Superior Publishing LLC.

Contents

1	The Unimaginable	1
2	Never Say Never	5
3	Broken Vows	9
4	Tangled View	12
5	Temporary Closure	16
6	Insecurities	19
7	Lowly Place	23
8	Ungodly Paths	26
9	Averted Face	30
10	Revisited Past	33
11	Undesirable	37
12	Breaking Point	41
14	True Stance	52
15	Changes	56
16	Painful Wait	61
17	Second Invitation	65

18	Battlegrounds	70
19	The Fall	75
20	Sin No More	79
21	Epilogue	84

Copyright © 2021 by Prophetess Nekeshia Gibson

All rights reserved. No part of this book may be reproduced in any manner whatsoever without written permission except in the case of brief quotations embodied in critical articles and reviews.

Superior Publishing, 2021

I

The Unimaginable

Life has a way of counteracting what a person may speak or possible think regarding the things they would not do concerning themselves. Often, we perceive things that goes against what we believe or think, and it causes us to react in ways that could be considered values. These values are often taught by those who walk in them or the instinctive values that allows one to know right from wrong. The instinct stresses those values and allow those who experience it to feel a form of regret for going the route we already knew was not right. Once this value is crossed that one puts in place for themselves, it is not an easy thing to revisit and causes a person to question what they will or will not do. How is this possible you may ask? Well, if we go against one value we will not do, then who is to say we would not do it again and again and again. The emotional doubt begins to form into an actual visual force and the laughter of the enemy becomes louder. One thing I came to realize during these days would be just how much the enemy can hear when we speak out of our mouths what we will not do in respect to ourselves or others. Especially when it is connected to things you have seen and things that you have poor experiences in. After the death of my mentor, I found myself wondering in my thoughts what more could possibly go wrong. How much more could this shell of a person endure without becoming an occupant of the local mental ward. I had finally shaken loose from this abusive boyfriend who was incapable of expressing any form of compassion or empathy from the loss I had experienced concerning the many loved ones who were taken in a short period of time. The final straw being his unwillingness to be some form of comfort at the loss of my grandmother for a bottle and drugs. At that moment, I reached out to what was familiar to me. Even though I knew empathy would not be there, I instinctively reached out for what was familiar, and it expressed the emptiness that had always been there. Love was still something I desired so greatly from the opposite sex. It was the one thing I felt like I was missing and the last thing that wanted to be found by me. The source of those thoughts came from a manipulating spirit that was not finished in its hunger to destroy something that I had yet to realized was within me. After that last conversation with my now ex-boyfriend, I had come to a lower point within my life and dirt was my then current view. I did not see flowers, birds, and sunshine in those days that followed my loved ones' death. Only dirt, cracks, darkness, and a great loneliness that continue to invade my thoughts as well as my heart. Along with this view was a voice that was so very convincing in what it was saying to me and I found myself agreeing with it daily. After the death of the man of God, I found myself walking over to my grandmother's house practically daily and sitting in her driveway. I remember sitting there just having a conversation out loud with this voice that always seemed to respond with comments or questions to what I would say. It did not scare me nor was I questioning whose voice this was I heard as clearly as I could hear myself. It just felt nice to talk with whomever this was and not feel as if I had to justify my words, thoughts, or looks behind it. I remember thinking for just one split moment I found a peace that I had not really experience before. Sitting outside in the open space of the country, looking up at the sky, I knew simplicity for a brief second and it was okay. I remember thinking about the past years sitting there and how I ended right back in the place that terrorized me for as long as I could remember. The horrible dreams and nightmares flooded my thoughts during that moment. Enough to where I had to shake off the dread that was trying to move over me and steal that portion of peace I so needed in that hour. Grief was also a neighbor at that time, and it stood waiting for its chance to remind me of all that I felt like I no longer had. Truth be told, I resented how their issues was over and mine seemed continuous without paused. Yes, they were no longer present, but for my thoughts that had to be better than what I had come to call my life up until this point. What I had come to love was now inaccessible and the hollowness behind that thought was deeper than anyone could imagine. Even with feeling this way, this voice was a welcoming comfort in a time where I desperately needed to hear something relatable and feed the hunger to have someone listen regardless of who it was. There had to be someone who would listen to me for a change. I remember thinking this as I listen to this voice responding to my comments out loud and hearing a vehicle coming up the road. Never once did I think, never once did I imagine that outside of the voice talking, there was an ear listening and designated that moment to present to me the unimaginable of a promise I made that would soon be broken.

2

Never Say Never

Words are a powerful source that can bring about various situations and circumstances. When you do not know who you are or whose you are, you do not realize just how much words can be hijacked to be a weapon used against you or another person. Another aspect of the power behind words would be how they can travel down a line of generations to affect those then or later. Generational curses are real and hide until that moment in time to come into effect when you are not living a lifestyle covered under the blood. Being raised by a single parent, I never got to know my father growing up and only knew the male role model of my grandfather. Losing him at a very early age brought about a remorse that I know now was a moment for the enemy to use as a valuable weapon against me and my emotions. So, when I learned who my father was, I was too young to make that necessary connection both mentally and emotionally for a void I was yet to know was there. Filling that void was something I began to seek as I grew and learned the differences between sexes. Even through all the traumatic experiences I had been through, being loved was still in the forefront of my mind and my heart. I was watching the people I cared about finding a partner, but here I was still alone in every capacity a woman could feel when she does not love herself. Sitting outside my grandmother's house, that thought fell on my mind bringing forth a sadness that was overwhelming to the point tears began to fill my eyes. I remember speaking this to a God I still had not come to know as He wanted me too and not realizing that the enemy was gleeful to introduce to me that which I had proclaim I would never do. I heard a vehicle coming up the road and glanced in that direction without really having interest in who it was. Seeing that it was someone I vaguely knew; I threw my hand up in acknowledgement with a small smile and little interest or thought. I watch the vehicle slowing, stopping, and backing up to the end of the driveway. Curious to what this person wanted, I wondered if they were just speaking due to the passing of my grandmother. Not quite understanding what they were saying from a distance, I got up to walk towards the end of the driveway to hear them. I remember him asking how I was doing and giving his condolences to the passing of my grandmother. I thanked him and smiling preparing to turn and go back to my chair to finish my conversation with the voice. Seeing this motion, he began a small conversation with me by asking what I was doing. I believe the look on my face must have informed him that I did not feel this was his business and he quickly cleared that up with how cold it was to be out. I informed him I liked the cold and then answered him with why I was sitting outside. Slowly the conversation moved forward, and we sat talking for a good while. It felt good speaking with someone of the opposite sex that held intelligent conversation and did not make me feel as if I needed to dumb down. The problem though would be the mindset that was already there and the line that should never be crossed. After he left, I remember going back to my chair, sitting down, and smiling from the interaction. Going over the conversation and being grateful for human-to-human contact even in the simplest way. At that time, I did not know that the enemy uses the simplest things, the smallest pleasures, to setup a trap you would miss if you were not watching. But how can you watch, how can you know when you neither had the right form of relationship with the one who can expose it? It is possible, but when another voice comes in agreeing with the desire and not what is right, you will tune the reasoning out. At that moment, sitting there, reasoning was barely heard and barely influential. As the days went by, I began to sit outside my grandmother's house with less anticipation for talking with this voice and more for one-on-one interaction with this new person. Practically each time I was out, he always managed to pass by as if he knew I was out there and knew I was waiting. Each interaction was different, and each brought about a desire to see them again. Simplicity became interest and now interest was evolving rapidly into something else. Within a matter of weeks, we were talking on the phone and the void was being filled. Or so I thought. Conversation went to laughter and laughter was introducing my emotions to a place I had always thought I would never step into. It is amazing what a person will swear they will never say, never go, and never do until it is presented to them. It will come wrapped up in the very thing a person long for and quietly position itself as a gift that truly is sent just for you. I became comfortable in the presence of this man and closed every door, window, or mailbox that truth was trying desperately to impart into me. My mind did not care that this was not right. My flesh did not care that this was wrong. My eyes did not care that they could see the truth, but my heart knew. And that was the one place I could not ignore no matter how hard I tried. I crossed a line that broke the last thread within me and now my title turned from girlfriend to mistress. Despite my attempts to turn a blind eye to my actions, my steps were now positioned for a downhill journey that would not lead to the changes I thought would take place.

3

Broken Vows

 Image is something that many ponder over when they encounter people, a place, or a thing. However way one presents themselves to outsiders would be how people think on them during and after that encounter. The presentation of themselves and the words that they use can be the foundational point of what people think and, oftentimes, what they consider themselves to know about a person. Unfortunately, images can be a persona of what an individual considers themselves and is not always the truth of the matter. It is easy to say many things, but not always easy to live up to what has been spoken. This is something I began to face when I entered a space that was too cramp for me, but I wanted to believe there was a place or, better yet, room for me to exist. Though my mind tried to see an alternative picture that showed only two people in this space, it was obvious that there were three people in it, and I was not in the forefront. I would always be in the back and there was no contest in that. So use to being second or last in pretty much everything, I tried to find comfort in just being with someone. But how can I find comfort in an uncomfortable position that was pulling me more and more into an awkward space. I remember thinking that maybe just maybe he would see how good I would be for him and ignoring how bad he really was for me. Daily I remembered how I made a promise to myself and spoke to others that I would never put myself in this position. That I would never be the reason another woman cries, or a family is torn apart due to my actions. There was not a day I was not reminded of my words, but my flesh was finally getting something I so long desired. Even though it was not rightfully mine. I knew one day I would have to contend with this, but at that moment it was the furthest thing on my mind. I had attention, I had communication, I had laughter, and that part of me who cried out for these things was now getting it. I tried to believe this could go on for a while. That I could be satisfied with a part of him. Not knowing at that moment that the part I thought I had was truly only a piece. A piece that eventually shown itself to be the space that was too cramp for me to enter. About three months into this situation, I began to dream more but they were different. I remember one dream where I was running for my life in my mother's house and found myself trapped in the living room. Turning I saw the tall form of a black draped figured standing near the window and door. My escape route was blocked, and I could feel my heart racing trying to figure out how to get away. Suddenly the figured removed its hood and I saw what had been chasing me all my life standing before me. Sneering at me, it let me know without moving its mouth it would always chase me no matter where I go. Waking up, I was terrified and, in the dark, felt the presence of a malevolent force that waited for me to go back to sleep. Looking around the room, the feeling of fear once again became a blanket wet and cold wrapping around me. I laid there trembling in fear and shaken to the core. When would these things stop happening to me? How could I make them stop? This night followed me for weeks and nothing assisted with alleviating the terror that seemed to find me when nighttime came. I remember speaking on the phone with my cousin, who was more a sister, about the different situations going on concerning dreams and this relationship. I was grateful because once again I had someone to talk with and she listened without interrupting. I had started sharing with her the dreams and various other situations that I was dealing with. She was hardcore and basically gave me the truth. But she never doubted me and the things that I shared with her. I remember her asking me to come back to church and expressing how she believed I would be a great help with the children. I did not think this was a good idea but gave my word I would consider it. There were different factors that came into play when considering me returning to the household of faith. The biggest being the lie I was living with a man who would never treat me anymore than what is on the side of a plate. I remember waking up one Saturday morning and deciding to go sit over at my grandmother's still vacant house. Walking over there, I had no thoughts of seeing this man, but hearing the voice that I had long ago stopped interacting with. I remember grabbing a lawn chair and moving it to my spot in the driveway. Closing my eyes, I spoke silently in my mind to see if the voice would respond to me. Waiting for an answer, I looked up at the sky and saying I am sorry directly to it. I had messed up. I had gotten on a path that was inexcusable and I knew I needed help to fix what was completely shattered. I needed help with climbing out of the pit, but I never saw the trap the enemy was yet setting for me to stumble once again.

4

Tangled View

Time has a way of slipping pass you and sneaking up on you when you least expect it to. One minute can feel like an exaggerated hour and a month can feel like an excruciating year. Knowing this type of feeling or thought, one can never prepare themselves with what could possibly happen day to day. You just wake up hoping beyond hope that on this day something good will happen. Something in your world will be better and eliminate the thoughts that are never far from your mind that worst will take place prior to the end of the day. During this time, my days were sad, but my nights were exactly what they had always seemed to be. Nightmarish. After that day in my grandmother's driveway, the voice did not speak or acknowledge me. I remember going back several times and yet no response was given to me for the encouragement I was seeking. At this point, this relationship was ending, and, in some ways, there was relief that it was. But the loneliness was rising and refusing to be by itself even when it was the best thing for me during those times. Now I understand that entanglement desired to keep me just like

I was and working closely with the advisory to promote bondages that would cancel any form of living I sought. The time together was gradually getting shorter, and depression was moving in to show it had never left in the first place. I remember considering returning to the household of faith and could not really identify with why. Everything I had done up to that point was too embarrassing to think on and acknowledge that there was one who saw it all. Though I recognized that thought, the worst was the fact that there could be others who saw or knew what I had done. Shame is a powerful emotion, and it also hangs around just to distort one's view even more so that they can continue to walk in bondage. No, I had not done this alone, but I was a willing accomplice who allowed emotional dysfunctions to have a voice in my actions. It was unrealistic for me to believe that someone else's life could be mine just as it is for mine to be someone else's. Regardless of these facts, I had made room for another issue to take up camp in a place already filled to the rim with disasters. I remember having a dream that showed me washing inside of a pool in a temple before walking down this beautiful adobe white hallway. This hallway led me to a door and another pool that I entered with the assistance of a person that seemed to be waiting on me. When I woke up from that dream, a voice told me to return to church and not be afraid to go. It was the fall of 2008 and things were challenging for my heart. A few weeks after this dream, I decided to return to church, but had no intentions of doing any more than sitting in the back just listening. Every Sunday I would get up and go to regular service, but something in my heart knew I was supposed to be doing something different than what I was. I remember the youth department head approaching me and asking me would I consider working with the young people. In all honesty, I was shocked that this assignment was being offered to me. Especially with the fact I had not been coming that long, but she let me know she felt that I would be good for the kids. I agreed to come and view one Wednesday night without giving a direct answer of yes. In many ways I wanted to say no, but in the end accepted to come sit in. I shared this with my eldest child who informed me that she believed this was a good idea. Curious to why she felt this way, she let me know that she felt I was good with kids and related to them well. I remember sharing this with this man I was gradually moving away from daily. I had gotten to the point where calling was no longer interesting and the lengthy time of not seeing each other did not matter. His reaction was shocked with a hint of why I would consider this. I remember thinking was it because I would be working with children or the fact that people would know. I did not pose that question to him and in that moment, I decided to attend that Wednesday's service. I remember going to the class and listening to what was being said to the children. Before I knew it, the department head introduced me to the class and handed it over to me without me knowing what was going on. I was shocked and trying to figure out what in the world was I supposed to do. Standing at the podium, I introduced myself and asked the children to share with me their names and the things they liked about the class. One thing led to another and I taught the class for the remaining of the time. I remember after the class was completed the department head asked me again would I teach for now on and positioning to me the offer of head teacher. This was a complete surprise that this was being offered to someone like me. I agreed to think about it and left to go home still in disbelief of what had taken place. After getting home, I thought over the night and found that I was happy with everything that had happened. I knew that this was a chance to do something good, but the dirt I had on me caused me to fear what could happen if people knew things about me. I knew I had to change, and I knew I needed to stop with everything that was not right. Though my heart felt like it was breaking, I now know it was the heart of the flesh that was screaming no and unwilling to come out of what it was clinging to. The next day, I decided not to contact this man and let him just go without explanation or anything. Enough was enough. I had eyes watching me and it did not look right for my children to grow attached to someone who was involved in a lifestyle that reflected differently from what I was teaching them. I knew I was never going to be more than a visitor. It is amazing how a small amount of time can generate the greatest amount of pain even when you rarely have the view before you. Pain had switched to comfort, but the pain had not really left. It was only covered up with a shallow grave waiting to be felt in its intensity all over again. I dove into working in this youth department as if it were a single grasp of a lifeline that had been offered to one who had moved into the deepest of waters. I pushed every thought that had been in the front to the back and crammed anything associated with this new journey in front of it. But there was no escaping the past and there was no escaping the truth. No matter how much you bury something, if it still had life any way, shape, or form, the possibility of resuscitation is there regardless of how long one thinks it is dead.

5

Temporary Closure

    Obligations come in various forms and different positions for every person who walks on this planet. With each one introduced to a person, the amount of purpose is demonstrated and implemented to ensure the results are befitting the moment. Every obligation materializes something and that something can be a reflection off the individual completing it no matter what it is. There is a particular movie that comes into my thoughts when I began writing this chapter and that movie would be Forrest Gump. In one scene, Forrest is sitting speaking with a nurse while eating out of a box of chocolates and shared with her how his mother said "life is like a box of chocolates. You never know what you're going to get." That jumps out at me because during this point, I believed I had picked a specific chocolate that had never been sampled nor experienced in my life. Working in this youth department had become a medication like penicillin for me. It felt as if the things in my life up to that point were slowly dissipating and this new experience was now shifting what I formerly knew. Peace was still not something I had obtained, but fear was no longer dominating my days as it once had. I remember purchasing different materials to put together for Wednesday night's teaching for the children. There was a mixture of ages present on those nights and I knew I needed to compose things that would affect all of them at once. Every week, I was blessed with different ideas, different topics, and different comprehension skills for the lessons that seemed to flow from me. With each presentation, the department head and the pastor were in agreement once I explained the purpose that each would be positioned to gain from the youth. I felt a sense of worth as I became more involved with the children and this department. It allowed me to become active within the church and offered the opportunity for me to be used outside of just this department. Life seemed be different and developing in a way I never thought it could go in. With a purpose and a mission that looked like what I had hoped, but different in the way it moved. Though life seemed to be improving for me, the inside was slowly beginning to talk. The more I pushed it to the side, the louder it was growing, and it refused to be completely silent. The loneliness and self-worth were collaborating to remind me that I yet had received what I wanted in life. That was that scope of love and acceptance that was right before me, yet I was still unable to touch. My thoughts gradually started reviewing how, even though I was not completely happy, I still had someone to talk at if not to. I remember still pushing those thoughts away, but my strength in the push was not as forceful as it once was. I began comparing myself to the women I had started interacting with in the church and found so much of myself in shortcomings to what I saw. The eyes can be deceived, and the mind will bring forth illusions that are not there. Where low self-esteem will see beauty, strength, happiness, prosperity, etc., the truth will show you everything opposite of the illusions. During that time, I had no idea of the incredible number of illusions my mind and flesh had around me. All I knew, everyone had what I truly believed I wanted for myself and my flesh was ensuring I realized this. No amount of diving into the youth department could detour my thoughts, but I made sure not to neglect what I had been charged to do. For months, I walked around every week battling in my mind and battling my flesh to get the form of peace that was simply going away. Even though all of this was going on, the dreams were still there and were growing in ways that kept me on edge. The intensity of them caused nervousness because I never knew what would happen daily behind them. I remember having a death dream of a person I knew and waking up to find out they had passed that morning. It was nerve wrecking to know this before it happened, and I was desiring someone to explain to me what was going on. I was still sharing a few of my dreams with my cousins, but the depth of them I kept to myself with hopes that sooner or later I would find someone to explain. I remember the sadness I felt that the man of God was no longer around to help me figure out what was going on and why my dreams were happening in the way that I was being shown. The fight to understand these dreams, the hiding within the youth department, and the resisting of my thoughts, as well as emotions, were slowly tearing down my strength. With this happening, the past came rushing back at me in the forms of the ex-men who had encamped too long in my life, but the desire to have someone did not care. I bartered with my own self in the attempt to not walk backwards with the very things that had contributed to my destruction. I resisted with every molecule of my makeup and dug my heels in when I felt myself being dragged back into my past. Not realizing that the finale of my past had a new chapter added to it and this time the battle was bigger than I could ever imagine.

6

Insecurities

One thing that a person cannot escape is themselves. This one spot can bring about various thoughts, but it can never be replaced despite one's attempts to do just that. Reality will come in and remind you of who you are, where you are from, what you have done, and where you are heading. If you are not careful of which side of the field, you are operating on and playing for. People can paint a picture, but if it does not fit the reality, it is simply the imagination. Some realities are hard to face, some are difficult to accept, some are emotionally damaging, but no matter what it is the reality of one's life. No one has the capability of knowing what their realities will look like once they are born, but they have a choice on how they handle it. I could have faced my life head on and made the choices to go opposite of what I knew. The problem was emotionally I was still tied to my past and had allowed myself to believe this what I knew was reality. There were still many things I had not tried and had no desire to try. Thinking on this, I know now it was not because I could not, but there was still a small drop of value that was still deep down on the inside. Daily memories were pouring back in and my thought pattern felt completely broken. I was still suffering in ways I could not express without feeling childish and presenting on the outside what others desired to see. Yes, it felt extremely wonderful to be looked upon as smart, knowledgeable, and kind. But the inside was wrecked, hurting, broken, and barely functioning on life support. I remember lying in bed one night pondering over the lesson plan I had completed for the coming up Wednesday class. Thinking over the material and the information I had pulled out to teach. I could not understand at that time how I was able to compose lessons from the Bible, but I was always thinking over the scriptures that were being discussed. That night I fell asleep watching television and once again the dreams came forth. That night I remember dreaming on the household of faith I was in and seeing a lot of things taking place that were not good. I woke up wondering about what I had saw in my dreams. It was different from how I normally dreamed and this time it felt as if I was standing in it watching what was going on. All the next day I wondered about this dream and could not shake this feeling that was coming over me. The next night, I dreamed again, and it was like the previous one with some differences. I remember thinking about both dreams and how they came right behind each other. That nervousness was intensifying, but I could not comprehend what was going on. The third day, I remember thinking about going to sleep that night and if I would dream again. I knew without anyone having to tell me both dreams were connected and they both had something to do with the household of faith I was in. All that morning, I wondered on those dreams and wished there were someone I could speak with right then. My cousin was at work, so there was no way to speak with her to get her thoughts on what these dreams were saying. All that morning on the third day, I pondered and pondered these dreams until right before my eyes I saw a familiar person pop up in my mind. I knew this was the person to reach out to and immediately I contacted them. After telling them why I was calling, I shared with them the two dreams I had the past couple of nights as well as the feeling of dread that was slowly growing within me. I let them know I did not understand what any of this means and for some reason I saw them in my thoughts knowing to call them. After speaking with me, I was told to ask God what it was He was telling me before I went to bed that night. Being specific and wait to see what it was He wanted me to do. Ending the call, I rolled over the conversation in my mind, but it did not relieve that dread growing inside of me. I did not know what the answer would be or even if I would get one. All I knew was something was happening, and I knew there was nothing I could do to stop it. That night, I remember lying in the bed feeling afraid to follow the instructions I was given. My entire being was scared because of the interaction that possibly would take place, but I also knew there was no way to avoid it. Closing my eyes, I whispered and asked God what it was He wanted to tell me. Lying very still., I waited for a response, but never got one. Exhaling a huge breath, I closed my eyes partially relieved I did not hear anything and partially hurt because of it too. I honestly do not remember falling asleep, but that night I had another dream. This time, I stood outside the household of faith and it was pitch black. I remember walking on the inside and seeing lights on, but there were very few people within. I remember walking back outside and seeing many people out there, but they were so dark and not moving. Just standing around outside the doors. I remember looking up and seeing this form sitting on the roof of the household of faith with its leg dangling over the edge while the other was bent at the knee. It looked around at the people laughing outside before looking at me. Suddenly I heard a voice speak to me and it gave me a message. It told me the names of three people to go to with all three dreams and tell them exactly what he was saying. I woke up and saw that it was morning. Feeling as if that one dream consumed my entire night and feeling as if it was burned into my mind. Every word I remembered and everything I saw. I remember calling the person who had given me the instructions and told them about the dream. I shared with them the three names I was given, and they told me to be obedient to what I was told to do. I remember calling all three men and telling them I was told to call with this message. I began telling each one that a voice told me the church doors would be closed and feeling afraid to tell them. Though I felt this way, I could not relay the dreams without completing what I was told to do and to say. There was the pressure inside of me every time I attempted to cut parts out causing me to speak what I was told. The last person I was told to go to would be the most difficult because of the stance they had within the house. I remember telling them exactly what I dreamed all three nights and the message given on the third. I remember hearing their laughter and dismissing what I had shared with them as just a dream possibly connected to what I had ate or watched. I felt crushed behind this interaction because I desperately wanted to understand what was going on with me and why my dreams had changed. Though the answers did not come from the source I thought it should come from to explain to me what was happening. I remember hanging up the phone still hearing their laughter in my ears and feeling that same low place come even closer than where it was. Today I can admit I was wounded from the interactions and on that day, the enemy positioned defeat for a territory he was sure was his from that day forward.

7

Lowly Place

    Wisdom is not a portion we are automatically born with or walk in. Each person can obtain their portion of it, but it must be sought after to be gifted in it. Unfortunately, it is something that many feel they walk in already connected to various age groups of either gender. Even though this is the thought it does not mean it is an accurate one. Everyone feels they are making the best choice for their lives, at that moment. But if you are moving in life without the proper and truthful connection that can only be obtained in a relationship with Christ, your movements are in vain and the possibilities of errors are greater. Maturity is also a source of growth and development in positive ways. Though the fruits of its inheritance are not always sweet to ingest, it is still a portion of growth that many times accompanies wisdom. This was yet not a place I knew nor an inheritance I had obtained. True I had learned a lot in my short time of living, but those two identities I had yet obtained. It was grace and mercy that was keeping me during those dark times. Even then it was not anything I had did or was doing that caused this to be extended over my life. Days had begun to pass after relaying the messages I was told to do, and I could feel the subtle changes towards me. I started disconnecting from the church again, but I still desired to work with the children. I felt that empty feeling even the more as I looked around seeing people with each other. I was still living in my mother's house and it was slowly taking a toll on me. I remember going shopping with my cousin and was happy to get out of the house. I felt confined and little by little depression was creeping back causing me to cave into my thoughts. I remember being in a particular store when someone she knew came in looking for her. I knew she was loved and popular with many people which was not a surprise being the type of person she was. I heard her talking to someone and walking up the aisle looking for them to see if she was finished. Upon reaching them and seeing who she was talking with, I found it was someone she had been friends with for a very long time. I did not know them only what she had shared, so my only response coming up to them was saying hello. I remember seeing the look they gave me and immediately I turned to walk off. The last thing I wanted and needed was to become entangled in anything again. I was tired of the confusion and desired only peace with a smidge of happiness. Anything else I was not looking towards. I remember walking down another aisle in the store waiting for them to leave or us. Seeing that she was ready to go, I averted my eyes from her friends and ignored the looks from both parties. Returning to my mom's house, I considered doing the lesson for the following week. Though it was on my thoughts, it was numb on my heart and I found myself creeping into self-pity. During that time, it felt like a safe place, but it was really preparing me for much more than I could see or know at the time. Behind my eyes were thoughts of previous relationships and a previous lifestyle that I had not yet fully left behind. Though I was active in church with the teaching of the children, the old man was yet still alive and kicking. She had not died and had a whole lot to say. At that point, I was very attentive and listening silently with no arguments to every word being spoken. There were two people operating at that point. One was teaching and the other was dying. Thinking back on that period of my life, I know now it was God continuous breath keeping me alive and not allowing me to suffocate in my own fleshly mess. The mind can truly be the devil's playground when you have nothing to anchor it in The Lord and the words He has spoken. There are those who will argue that it is natural to desire happiness and a life partner. Yes, this would be true to those who are rationalizing this with themselves, but for those like me. You can not receive something if your life is still more connected to the natural man than it is to the spiritual one. I had people I was talking to, but that is exactly what that was. People talking to the desires and not to the spirit. During those times, the desires of my heart were more flesh than anything else, so seeing passed this was not an option. My mind steadily agreed that no one could understand where I am and how I was feeling. This left me open to consider happiness wherever it came from and from whomever was willing to offer it to me. I stopped considering other people's feelings and the hurt that I could possibly bring upon them. Life had been so very cruel in too many ways for me not to opt to be just as cruel in return. The dreams and visions were still consistent in how they were coming with the different things I was seeing. They left little room to doubt what they were sharing in every detail on all levels. Life can be peculiar when you do not have the tools to understand what is going on and where it is leading. I knew I was in a very low place, but never could I have guessed that there was another level down to go.

8

Ungodly Paths

Every road that one takes leads to a place they are seeking or unwittingly discovered by accident. Each one will either be enticing to a person's desires or destructive to their very being. However way one chooses to look at it, paths are permanently connected to us and the courses we take in our lives. Now some paths people come to make a familiar setting or route, if you may, that they have decided they prefer to stay upon without any regards towards change. Some paths are introduced by familiar spirits that are designed to ensure the right ones are delayed or sometimes forgotten amid what is designed to pleasure the flesh. While suffocating the spirit in the hopes of what is found in it will never be discovered. The mind is a deep well of thoughts and emotions that goes beyond comprehension of just how much it all flows within the very depth of one's inner man. When a person is trapped in their mind with their past, something offered that relatively looks better than what they knew, becomes acceptable in the presentation. That is where one loses focus on what is the truth versus the reality of what cannot be changed. Focus is the primary target under attack and once this is stolen, it is easy to become mislead by the desires that grow in magnitude in one's own mind. I was still active in the youth department and found some relief with this part of my life. The time spent teaching was a wonderful feeling, but I had yet experienced the evolving of from flesh to spirit. My meaning by this is, my flesh had not become subject to The Spirit, so it was actively still talking and desiring what it had always desired. I remember getting a call one night and being told that someone was interested in me in a personal way. Curious, I asked who this person was and found an excitement in just knowing that someone looked at me this way again. I remember being told they wanted my phone number to speak with me directly, but out of respect the one telling me this did not want to give this information out without my permission. Asking again who this person was, I waited in anticipation and excitement to even consider a legitimate relation with possibilities of what I had always wanted. But the excitement was short lived when it was shared with me who this new interest or secret admirer really was. I remember my heart dropping and closing my eyes in disappointment. This was yet not a place I wanted to revisit nor a place I wanted another invitation from. Regardless of the reasons, I still had those values that I could not ignore for hopes of something greater. I am a true believer that what is for me is for me, but life as well as the enemy were beginning to convince me that maybe what is for me was stuck where it was not meant to be. These words were whispered into my thoughts and I found myself intrigued with what it was convincingly insinuating to my mind. In the beginning of this chapter, I stated that some paths are placed before you to delay one from those that are right. It is not because they will not happen, but position to make the way more difficult when the time comes to choose the life you really want to live. I remember listening to what was being stated to me and the thoughts begin to congregate in my mind. My fleshly heart was crying out for attention, for love, for conversation and slowly an appeal began to form. I agreed to speak with this man and gave permission for numbers to be exchanged. Thinking is it possible to find happiness with someone who was unhappy in their situation or is it just words being stated to satisfy a thirst that would never be filled no matter how far one looks in their situation. I begin to rationalize this new introduction to my life and the thoughts that this is as good as it was going to get for me settled on my thoughts. For some reason, it seemed as if I either attracted those who abused me physically/mentally and now those who were already married to another person. During those times, I could not make the differences out to what was really going on in my life. I was beginning to accept that the only happiness I would possibly have would be that which was already started somewhere else. I was now the person I had turned my nose up to and spoke with complete disgust about. I was the other woman, and this was the identity I felt would be the final look I would have. I remember my phone ringing about fifteen or thirty minutes later from a number I did not recognize. Seeing this number, a voice let me know this was the person who sent me the message. I knew, in that moment, I could just not answer or stand my ground in strength I perpetuated to have during those days. I remember thinking in my mind that I would not allow sweet words or issues they claimed to have at home to convince me to go this direction. I really felt and thought I had the ability to shoot down flattery or even tone from brainwashing me into a place I knew was not right. Answering the phone, I prepped myself to be distant in introduction and limited in conversation. I let them know I was told they were interested in me and wanted to get to know me. I remember informing them that I did not believe in being involved with a man already committed to another person and let those words be my stance. I listened to them saying they understood but would like to still be friends if nothing else. I remember pondering over those words and thinking that was innocent enough while at the same time a small voice yelled walk away. Though I heard this small voice, the loneliness was louder and the accompanying yearning to interact with the opposite sex. I did not weigh any options for my decision. I considered myself mature enough to hold my grounds and be a friend even though the heart wanted so much more. Accepting this arrangement, if I can call it that, we began a conversation that was normal in its presentation. But there was an undertone that stood in the background with clear intentions of not being ignored. Even with seeing this, I remained confidence that I had everything under control regardless of anything he tried to say. Illusions can be real when one has not faced their demons and the spirits that accompany them. The spirits come to set the trap with familiarity due to their knowledge learned over the course of years they have worked to entrap a soul. The illusions are shifted, adapted, and upgraded to make the next trap more enticing, more inviting, and more desirable to the one searching for it. I remember getting off the phone with the thoughts that I am finally in control. Smiling, while looking at my television, with little awareness that the path introduced this time would lead to a destination I had thought long gone.

9

Averted Face

    There are some things people do not have the desire to look upon and makes the decision not to. Whether a television show, movie, home environment, work environment, or situations unfolding before them, people make a conscious decision to turn their heads to anything unpleasant to them or situations that attempt to distance themselves from. Each situation is different, but the underline reasoning behind the motion can be linked to where that person is at that time. One situation that can be connected to the averting of the head would be the illusion of love. This four-letter little word has so much power in how it is felt whether in a positive way or a negative way. Even though I had my children at that time, I still had not experienced the positive effects of love or the true affects that it provided. I could not explain it because it had never been demonstrated towards me personally in a relationship. I had felt the love of those who were no longer in the land of the living, but that desire of the heart had not been fulfilled. How could one explain this four-letter word when they only read about it in novels connected to make believe people during a make-believe time? It is not possible. Human to human connections is not easily to make in a world positioned to strip you and not build you. So, to understand this word in the true depths of its meaning had simply not come to be in my life during those times. I thoroughly enjoyed working in the youth department, but the desires of the flesh were still prominent in its hunger to have what I saw everyone else as having. The inner emotional pain was surreal, and it was not easy to simply ignore it or the weight. The walls were beginning to develop cracks in my mind allowing past experiences to come to the forefront with little effort. Depression was still having its pillow talk with me and had a constant reminder of life's disappointment. Reality was simply silent and only offered its advice when it felt it had little choice. So, the comfort of looking the other way was just another means to cope and agree with what had come to be my life during those times. It was now late summer of 2009 and August was right around the corner. I had begun to desire my own place and space for a life I felt I wanted again. My conversation with this new man was still practically daily and my delusions of love began to bloom in my mind. I ignored the stance I so strongly positioned in the beginning of the conversations and slowly began to grasp those shallow strings of a promise I thought was before me. I remember he had to go away for a while and my thoughts were difficult to perceive this. I now realize this was time positioned for me to choose to do that which was right, but had yet to move in. If this were all the happiness that I would have then so be it was my mind frame. One thing that is difficult for a lost soul to realize is no matter how good you position yourself to be for a person, it does not mean it is for that person. You are only feeding a natural life that never had a chance to be more than just that: flesh. The other person can never really see what is before them when it is established in sin and with compensation of flesh. After being told he was leaving for a few weeks, I began to desire my own place even the more and a job to cover the expenses associated with it. My mind had started reasoning with my actions and I rationalized that if I position something different on his return it would make life with me more appealing. I wanted to be completely different in the eyes of this man. Even if it changed my appearance to myself. This was something different in my mind even though similar characteristics were standing tall in its presentation. I could not see those resemblances that were so uncanny in how they stood out. My face was averted to what it all really looked like, and I fought hard to keep my eyes turned away from the truth. I remember dreaming the day after he left and seeing myself falling with nothing around me to prevent it. I fell for so long that once the impact came, I jumped up in my bed screaming. I remember shaking and feeling my heart beating as if it would break through my rib cage. Lying back down I thought on the feel of the impact and the shock behind it. I laid there afraid to go back to sleep and confused to what this dream was showing me. I could not rationalize in my mind what I was seeing, but the truth was not long in my future to what was to come. Life did not care about how it presented itself to me or whether I wanted to see it or not. No matter how long my face stayed averted, eventually I would have to face what was standing before me.

10

Revisited Past

    The river of time never stops and always travels regardless of where a person is in their life. Movement is constant and is not always consistent to what we want nor to what we feel. This river does not forget who it is associated with and it also does not allow its flow to shift or repeat despite the owner's desires. It pushes forth steadily unbothered by its surroundings or the emotional turmoil of the one it belongs to. It has a destination it must get to and for that reason it will never reverse its course. It had been several days since this new interest had left and for me it was a deadline I had associated to the departure. I began looking for a job with intensity for this happiness I began to think would become a reality. Fantasy was starting to look like an actual view I could see rather than think. Maybe was now a possibility. A faint wind was blowing, and my form of hope was being fanned by it. Though, during those times, I never question where this wind was coming from or why. I remember making the decision to put in an application for a job opening. A family member had told me they were hiring, and I felt this could potentially be the opportunity I had been waiting for. Not long after applying for a position, I received a call to come in for an interview and excitement was automatic for me. There were significant barriers before me, but I pushed forward with the hopes that it would work itself out. I did not consider my experience with these issues, just trusted it would work out. After completing the interview process, about a week later, I completed the second interview to receive the initial position information. I remember hearing the days I would be working and the hours that were associated with them. I realized how the hours clashed with not just church, but also with Wednesday nights bible study. I felt a moment of confliction, but like the other situations I had before me, I pressed on believing that this would work out as well. Never once did I consider the possibility that I should not take the position and look for something else. I had made the decision to go back to school online for my degrees and felt that this was the right move to do. The urge to go to college was working out so far and I felt that making the effort towards employment for my own place was the necessary move I needed to make for my small family. I remember the excitement I had knowing that it would not be long before I had my own place. Not only would I have my own space, but also a chance to demonstrate my abilities to be a good woman. So, I thought. I went to the department head for the youth and informed her I had just received new employment that conflicted with the hours for church service in both areas. I saw her disappointment and concerns towards the lessons every week since I was the one who did everything. I assured her I would complete a month worth of lessons plans for the remaining teachers so that they could continue the process, with hope I was able to come after my ninety days of employment. I began working on lessons that night and thinking how I would have to tell the children that week it would be a while before I was able to return to the class. Many of the children I had become use to seeing every week and when I did not see them, I checked on them. Knowing that I would not see them for a while was hard to accept and a grief hit my heart. It never registered to me that I would feel this way about this department, about these children, until that moment I had to step away. I started considering turning the job down for something else that had hours that would at least work around the youth department. I remember shaking this off and rationalizing with myself. There were things I wanted to do and there was the chance that it may take even longer to secure another position for these things to come to pass. So, I shook off the melancholy, continue with the lesson plans, and prepared for a life I just knew I was about to enter. I remember my phone ringing while I worked on these lesson plans and heard my new friend's voice on the other end. Surprised, yet excited, I spoke with him for a little while before he had to disconnected. Hanging up, I looked at the phone with questions on my mind and in my heart. Questions towards the future and if it would evolve into the fairy tale I walked around believing for so long. I remember thinking that a small part of happiness was much better than the total lacking I had experience for far too long. Even in this consideration, I still refused to allow that door to open that was straining with the actual truth. I continue to hide in myth, fantasy land, or an alternate reality that the truth would be spoken. I remember shaking my head as if to clear it or push out the actual truth when it tried to penetrate my reality. I refused to welcome it and continue to add locks to the door that separated me from it. This was something and things were starting to look much better than I had ever known. I did not want the facts and made sure reality knew it can keep its truth. At that moment, destiny was in my hands and I felt I had a chance to see something much kinder that truth had never shown me. I dared truth to speak to me again and stepped even further into the life I wanted. It was so much so; I did not discuss this man with anyone outside of two people who

I knew wanted me to be happy. I had so little, I felt, during those times and something finally felt as if it was shifting to a place, I desired for so long with only a few kinks. Looking back now, I can see that walls were in place in my mind and scales had solidified over my eyes. Longing had turned into desperation and fear was the motivation behind it all. I never questioned what value I had for my own self and whether what I was receiving was associated to my self-worth. I only looked at my self-worth through the eyes of the one who was connected to me and attempted to be something valuable to them, not me. What they thought, what they stated, how they were to me was what had become a measuring cup of my own identity. I never ever assumed there was an identity that I had that was not connected to some man. Being with someone showed others and myself I am worth something to the world. But this was not true. Once again, I had reintroduced my painful past to my then present. A non-changing cycle that I had accepted was my life. Little did I know, a clock was being winded and eventual the hands would be allowed to move.

11

Undesirable

Purpose is not something one is given when they enter life and begin the process of growth. Once a particular stage is introduced into a person's life, the thought of purpose begins to form and eventually sought. Depending on the events that take place during that person's growth in life can either cause purpose to be sought even more or lost in the chaos of issues. Many times, in certain intervals of life, purpose can remind one of other's extensions in their life and it can be an unbearable thought. It can also show one just how far they have moved from that previous moment of time. Before starting my new position, my new friend was now called to go away for a longer amount of time. I remember feeling a great disappointment because the length was even longer than before. I remember making a promise that I would still be there waiting for their return and decided to take that time to move forward with my plans. I had begun working at my new job not long after he left and before long started to feel regret in the decision. The environment was overshadowed with an issue I had never thought would find me there. It is amazing when you think something is long over with and it reappears as if it had never left. I remember starting this job excited and motivated to see my dreams become an accomplishment. I remember going in with a drive and adding up paychecks before they came to begin the process of finding a new home. Though this was my determination entering into this new job, it was not long before it started slipping. I spoke to pretty much everyone in my work area, but there was one individual I had become a little friendlier with. He was a funny young man and we clicked immediately after a few conversations. So much so that we tried to take our lunch together just to laugh and gossip (remember I was not saved yet). I remember sitting in the lunch area with him and decided to broach a subject that had become noticeable to me whenever I came into work. I shared with him how a particular supervisor seemed to have a problem with me, and I could not understand exactly why. I remember sharing with him little things I had noticed when they worked with me and wondered if he possibly knew something about it. I watched him look down before glancing back up at me and knew he was debating on sharing with me what he knew. I gave him my word I would not repeat anything he shared with me and knew he believed me after a moment's pause. Finally leaning up, he shared with me what he knew and to my shock it was not what I was expecting. I remember him sharing with me that this supervisor was newly engaged, and this person was connected to my past. Hearing this, I sat back wondering who it was and why this was important to this supervisor. Looking at him, I asked him who was this person so that I could understand more clearly, if not confusingly, why this caused tension between me and them. I remember him telling me the name of this man in my supervisor's life and a sick feeling hit me hard in my stomach. Of all names that could have been stated, hearing my ex's name was the last thing expected. I remember flashes of my past with this ex coming into my thoughts and the horrible abuse I dealt with through his hands. I remember my co-worker seeing the look on my face and asking me what was wrong. Without thought, I shared with him some of the things that I had gone through at the hands of this man. I assured him she had nothing to be concerned about when it came to me contacting him and there was no desire for the opposite. My co-worker laid his hand on top of mine and his words of encouragement to not allow it to bother me. Even though I heard what he said and assured him out of my mouth, my thoughts knew anything connecting to this man around me would not be good. After that day, I would go into my new workspace with defenses up because it was becoming more and more tense for me. No matter how much I tried to respect this supervisor, it was becoming more evident that same regards was not being considered towards me. I remember my co-worker steadily encouraging me to ignore what was going on and just do my job for that day overlooking the things that were deliberately being done towards me. I had come so far from the person I use to be and felt myself slipping backwards to defend myself against an unwanted past unwanted memory. I remember feeling that maybe if I were still going to church some form of way it would help eliminate this urge to defend myself. I did not want to lose the chance to have the things I was working towards snatched from me due to a past I never wanted to remember or think upon. After a while, I went to the resource department and asked if it was possible to get Sundays off for church service. I knew it had not been ninety days but felt that it would not harm me to ask. I was denied this request and now faced a slippery slope that became difficult for my footing to keep traction to avoid sliding into an old place I had thought was forever covered. Walking to the break room, I was discouraged and slowly moving towards anger. I remember feeling how life had been so unfair in what it wanted to give me and how it always seemed determine to hurt me as much as it could. I slowly started feeling a spitefulness towards this man and this supervisor he was now engaged to. Now I know that at that moment I made up my mind to defend myself from these purposeful acts positioned to attack me. I refused to allow anything or anyone to come in between my goals and my purpose to have the life I had been denied for too long. I remember leaving off my break with a new stance for those who had just met me, but an old one I had sat down due to my surroundings. I made up my mind that I would not be a punching bag for this supervisor nor any other person who felt a need to provoke a reaction from me based on my past. A slow rage began to burn inside of me because I really came to think that life just refused to relinquish its hold on my happiness. Slowly the past started to merge with the present, but this time it would be different. This time I would not sit idly by and watch my happiness be tarnished by a past I fervently did not want to remember was back there. In my mind this time, I am going to stand my ground, display my strength, and return hit for hit if necessary. I remember my shoulders going back as I walked from the break room to the front and the hardness resurface to my face. In that specific moment, I made up my mind that being nice was just not a characteristic I could walk in and the last part of a gentle person was replace with iron that was positioned not to bend. Little did I consider that iron could bend when it was placed in the right fire which was not long down the road.

12

Breaking Point

Trauma is an experience that many would prefer to leave in the past where it is unable to do any more damage to a person. The problem with this concept, it is not always the best course of action to take for something that leaves a scar on your mental state far worst than your physical state. When one has a scar, they can see on themselves they take out time to find a way, or at least attempt to, improve the way that it looks to others and even themselves. Some people accept that it is a part of who they are, where they were, and are okay with others seeing what they survived. For those who have a scar mentally and emotionally it is not a pleasant experience to be reminded that it is there. When those scars are not examined, acknowledged, and healed, even with a scar to show proof that it was once there, they can become dangerous. Dangerous to the person who has them and those who find a way to pick at them without knowing that there is a festering wound that is infected enough to where it has now entered a dangerous point. Even with my time away from the past, the fact was it was there and very much alive within me. I knew that if a wall was scratched in my mind, it had the potential to cause a leak in what I had shut behind it. Thoughts surrounding this one particular ex were sensitive and unwelcoming for me. If I encountered people that knew I had a connection to him and they asked about him, I quickly answered to change the subject. That was a part of my life I was determined to leave right where it was. The problem was I never dealt with what I went through during that time or times prior to that. So much was built up in me and I did not realize that I was a ticking time bomb waiting for someone to mishandle me. I was not walking around looking for trouble, but the pain within me was waiting to strike out the first chance it got. After making the decision on that day in the break room not to be pushed around by anyone, that trigger had been pushed back to a place waiting to be released. I remember going into work some weeks later and a few of my coworkers would look at me with these strange expressions. Seeing this I brushed it off and went to the back to clock in for my shift. Many things had already transpired with comments that were positioned for me to find out this supervisor was stating. I remember walking to the front putting my badge around my neck and making the decision to ignore her as well as these comments. I realized I did not want anyone thinking I wanted to be in the place that she was in with this man. I knew what being with this man was like and wanted absolutely nothing to do with him. I saw this supervisor standing directly in front of the aisle I was coming up and I changed course to go the other way. I decided to go to another supervisor to see what station I was assigned to avoid her until she left for the day. Walking over to my station, I turned my light on and waited for my first customer to come. I saw that my new friend was working one station over and waved at him to get his attention. I remember him seeing me and shutting his light off to run over to where I was. I started thinking that he probable was coming to tell me a joke and smiled waiting to hear what he had to say. I remember him coming close to my face and telling me to watch out. Confused I looked at him puzzled to why he was telling me this, especially since I had just arrived. Seeing the look on my face must have told him I did not understand what he meant, and he leaned over to inform me that the supervisor dating my ex had intentions on getting me straight. Confused even more I asked him what I was supposedly getting straightened out about. I remember him telling me that it was stated I was in contact with my ex and the shock of this lie was mind blowing to me. I began to feel the trigger being released at that moment and the subtle rage turning into an ignited flame. At that moment I felt like a trapped animal in a cage that had finally busted through the latch. I reached pressing the key for the supervisor to come and position myself to confront this long antagonizing threat. My voiceless response must have informed my coworker the intents my actions had behind them because he immediately started talking to me to calm down and let it go. I could hear his words, they made perfect sense, but where I was at that point was beyond reasoning. I looked at him and told him I am tired of this past nightmare haunting my present. I looked towards the front and saw this supervisor walking towards my call. Positioning myself, I watched every eye at their station turning and waiting as if they already knew what was about to take place. I remember my coworker walking around my station to stand behind me and I knew he did this so that he could stop me if needed. Watching this supervisor, coming closer to where I was, I began seeing images in my thoughts towards what I wanted to do. Before I knew it, she was right in front of me and where I once felt rage was now a quiet calm. Looking her in her eyes, I asked her is there something she wanted to say to me or do? Standing my ground, I remember thinking of how tired I was having to defend myself over things that I no longer wanted or had any connections to. I remember her response being no and her walking away. In my thoughts, I realized that this game is not one I was willing to play, and I made my mind up that I never would again. I have put time and space between those times versus the time I was in a that moment. I had begun to think that it seemed almost impossible to move forward in life without having that part popping up whenever it liked. I wanted happiness for once in my life and I refused to allow the past to feel as if it had the right to associate itself with me any longer. I remember that entire day going by sluggishly. As if it were also tired of having to replay moments repeatedly. My coworker and I sat in the break room together practically quiet. I knew he was attempting to change the thoughts that were obviously going through my mind and attempting to dominate them. I remember him telling me some things that were going on with the current manager of that store. How the actions of one person seemed to make everyone in that workplace miserable without any thoughts or consideration towards others' feelings. Listening to him, I decided to participate in what he was attempting to do to make me feel better and take my mind off everything going on. I started speaking what came across my thoughts regarding the subject and now I know it was prophesying what was about to happen without me realizing what I was doing. I remember him laughing at my words and it snapped me from my thoughts. Looking at him laughing, I began to laugh myself and show him gratitude in being someone during that time I could talk with in what I was going through. I remember going back to my workplace aware that this supervisor and other employees were watching while laughing at me behind my back. Straightening my shoulders, I continue to do my job and not display anything related to fear or intimidation to a group of people who were closely resembling the things I had faced for so many years. In that spot, on that day, I felt more and more like the little girl who tried to fit in with a group of people that found more amusement in my misery than leaving me in peace. The world places weapons in one's hands without them ever knowing that they carry one. Once you accept that weapon it takes much more than strength to put it down and let it go. Looking back, I realized that the world's life is constantly evolving one enticed by it to dangerous levels that can overtake them if they allow it too.

Once you succumb to the trap you either believe what the world has to say about you, or you fight to find your truth. The truth that was positioned to me was not the one I was willing to accept nor believe. Clocking out for the night, my drive home was surrounded by thoughts of the entire day and the job. I wanted this to be a new moment, fresh with the promises of a new day ahead. Pulling up in front of my mom's home, I started wondering if what I am dealing with on this job is worth going through for a life I planned in my heart? Sitting there I remember thinking about the youth department and the simple joy I had even for a moment standing there teaching the children about the Bible. Getting out the car, I knew that if I allowed these situations to break me than the chances of me coming back together in even the smallest part was questionable. Walking towards the house, I decided to hold it together because the end would be worth it. Wouldn't it? Little did I know that the end I wanted would not be the ending I received, and the past was much closer that I could have ever believed.

13

Unsafe

    Walls are structures that are positioned to separate sections from one another. They can be beneficial when it comes to privacy, but they are also used to hide what many do not want to see or remember. Everyone can see the visible walls and understand the concepts towards what they are being used for. But those are not the walls that everyone hides behind or the walls that everyone can see. It is the invisible walls that many choose to build for the strength and sturdiness they seem to carry when one uses their own hands to structure them. When those walls begin to deteriorate or show signs of damage, one simply molds that spot back together until it starts falling apart again. It seems simple enough does it not, but there are significant issues that comes from this process. Invisible walls have no foundational point, so when they begin to crumble in one place it means there is structural damage closer to the source then one realizes. With this being the case, before one blinks, the thing they closed behind the original wall manages to show up out of nowhere. At that point, everything that is associated with the source comes through like a flood that has finally been released from behind the dam. The emotions, whether good or bad, ransacks the mind of the one who dared to push it into this place. Life at my workplace was becoming more and more difficult to enter without always having defenses up. The stress of working with this supervisor was taking a toll on me and I began to reflect this every time I came into the building. Several weeks after our initial interaction, I could tell that something was going on from the way she was reacting to my presence at work. I had chosen to ignore her up to this point, but the slight looks and responses my way caused me to search out what was going on this time. I remember going to my co-worker and asking him what has happened. Informing him that it was obvious something was up because of the way she reached towards me every time I needed something from a supervisor. I could tell he knew something but was debating on telling me about it. Smiling at him, I let him know it would be okay and he could tell me what he knew if he did know anything; in which I was sure he did. At that point, he looked up telling me that my ex was being released from jail the next day and my supervisor wanted me to know this detail. Staring at my co-worker, my mind flashed back to survival mode and a dread surrounded my very being. I did not know that he was incarcerated but felt that was the best place for a person like this. I did not care to find out what were the reasoning behind the situation, but felt this trapped emotion rise with a ferociousness. I saw the expression my co-worker had watching my response to this information. I attempted to smile at him, but knew it was a failed reassurance to him as well as for me. Finding my voice from deep down inside, I let him know it would be okay and I was not concerned about these details that he had reluctantly shared. I could tell he was not assured of my words and was grateful he did not say anything to press more from me. Sitting there, changing the topic, my thoughts went over the information I was just given. I began to prepare mentally for what could possibly happen and at the same time knew that it would. The remainder of the day was a blur of greeting customers, laughing with my co-worker, and pretending to be okay. It is amazing how emotions can be so energetic and at the same time draining. After making it home that night, I remember preparing for bed and for the next workday. I was not an everyday praying person, but that night I prayed so very hard that I never laid eyes on this man again. My night was restless and dreamless for the first time in a long time. Hearing the alarm that next morning, I felt as if I had just shut my eyes only for a brief moment. I made sure my children were ready and off to the bus stop before preparing to go in for the day. I remember shaking myself several times before pulling up into the parking area of my job. Reminding myself that I was no longer connected to this man and it did not matter what he was doing or who he was doing it with. As long as it was not me. I told myself this, but the emotions were leaking out faster than I was able to repair the cracks in my mind. I had been informed that the supervisor would not be coming in for the next few days and I should have been overjoyed to know this. But I was not. I knew without understanding how that they would be making an appearance. So, for my sake, I started building myself up to see and not see regardless of what was done. I started walking in and headed straight to the back into the break room until it was time for me to clock in. Seeing my new friend, I sat down with him and immediately went into a conversation to avoid the topic that everyone was discussing. I believed he realized my position and went along with it more in a helpful way. Walking out with him as he returned to the floor, I went back into the break room to mentally pump myself up. Watching the time, I prepared to clock in and spoke to everyone as if nothing were wrong or out of the ordinary. Going to the front to get my station for the day, I prepared my area for the customers that would come through my section. Time moved by relatively fast, and it almost seemed as if my prayers were being answered after all. I had only a few more hours to go before I was finished for the day and a slow excitement was trying to rise within me. I remember laughing with a customer when I felt someone tap me on my shoulders to get my attention. Turning to see who it was, my eyes saw something else before seeing the person attempting to distract me. The smile on my face froze and my heart slammed into my chest. In that moment of laughter, in that moment of turning, my eyes connected with one of the last people I wanted to see. I heard my name being called and finally moved my eyes to the person getting my attention, my co-worker. I knew my smile was stiff and I let him know that I am okay. Turning I continued checking my customer out and smiled telling them to have a good day. I remember my customer looking at me and stating, "I do not know what caused your posture to change but keep smiling. Do not allow anyone to steal your joy from you" before taking her receipt and leaving. In that moment, I realized that I could not let this man have this type of control over me. Turing back to my co-worker, I let him know I am good, and it would be okay. He looked at me, told me okay, and let me know he would hang around for a little while since his shift was over. I was immensely grateful for this act and expressed it with a hug right then. He stood there next to me talking with me to keep my attention focused on him and not the couple slowly making their way down to my section. I could hear the laughter and the celebratory comments as this newly engaged couple was making their grand introduction. I remember them walking up and pass my section with no words from my supervisor, but a hello from my ex. Calmly, with no expression but a simple smile, I said hello back and turned to continue my conversation with my co-worker. In that moment, the air was vibrating with many emotions from all parties, but I choose to ignore them all. The leak in my mind was now a stream pulsing from different memories of a horrific time I almost did not survive. I refused to let this wall break and mentally started pushing it back into place. Demanding it hold what was behind it and refusing to take no for an answer. Looking in my co-worker face, I remember him watching what was taking place behind me, but grabbing my hand squeezing it for reassurance. After a moment, he looked at me and told me they were no longer there talking amongst the other employees. I stood there smiling, but my physical form was shaking as if I was standing in a negative degree freezer with no warmth. I knew he felt this and responded by holding my hands tighter. I remember him asking me was the situation just that bad during those times and my only response was nodding my head. I could tell this disturbed him, so I let him know this was my past. Hearing my response, he just looked at me nodding his head to my comments while his face still showed his feelings towards it. At that moment, I regretted sharing the little I did, and I let him know that it was the past not my present. I watched him as he glanced behind me and saw the look on his face changed. He suddenly began talking loudly about something as if we had been doing this the entire time while moving closer to me. I looked at him momentarily confused about the swift change of subject, but understanding was not long in coming. I felt someone walk up behind me before moving past me slowly. Looking out the corner of my eye, I saw my ex walking past, lingering close by. Waiting. Looking into my co-worker face, I told him thank you with my eyes and I knew he understood. Though I was watching at him, I could see my ex staring, watching, signaling that he was there. For a second, I could feel the rage coming off him towards me and my unwillingness to give him a moment of my attention. Still looking in my co-worker's face, I watched as my ex positioned himself behind my co-worker's shoulder to get my attention. For a moment, our eyes met and from the look on his face, which was very familiar, I knew he was letting me know he was yet not through with me regardless of my position with him. Turning my head, I watched his fiancé approaching where he was positioned and realized safety was not as close as I thought it had been.

14

True Stance

Posture can be considered an outward and an inward position one takes for themselves. The outward position can be informative to another person looking upon it, but it takes much more to see the inward position. With the physical posture, it can look straight, bent, and sometimes even slouchy to others' review. Advice is naturally provided by those observing it, but it still takes the individual themselves to choose how they want to or even if they desire to change the appearance of it. For the inner posture, the same can be stated as far as if they want to change the look of it. A person's posture can be presented as perfect, but the inner one can be completely opposite of that frame. Eventually what is on the inside will begin to form on the outside and the look that was once perfect becomes as imperfect as that on the inside. The one thing that one has regarding this is a choice on how they want to position themselves. Not for others but for the image they desire to have for themselves. Choices are the one thing we all have in our lives for everything associated with our it. How we choose to implement them or even if we decide not to is truly up to us. After that day on my job, I began to earnestly look for my own place and move from where I was. One part knew this man was aware of my mother's location and would pop up when I was not watching. It was not long after that day and the looks shared that the phone calls began. I remember being off one night when this unrecognized number registered on my mother's phone and hearing this man's voice on the other end. Even though I stated clearly, I had moved on, the comments did not register with him. I knew after a few days that this would continue regardless of his situation and I had to do something to bring distance between us. The days had become longer since my new friend was still gone, and the waiting was unbearable. I really felt that if he were here that it would be less stressful and fearful for me during those times. My plans had not changed despite what was going on and I still had every intention on using the resources from this job to obtain the things I felt would lead to a safer happier lifestyle. My goals were getting my degree, getting my own place, getting transportation, and positioning myself as a perfect match for what I believed was the perfect match for me. Daily I chose to ignore my ex's attempts to slither back into my life and push back all the dread that came forth whenever he called or came to the job with or for my supervisor. During those times, it was obvious that the happiness that was there when he first came home was now questionable to those observing. I knew what putting on a show for outsiders was like being in that dysfunction of a relationship, so I recognized the strain of acting. A part of me began to feel sorry for her despite her actions and attitude with me. Watching them shed a lot of light on how I must have looked during those times where I was even unrecognizable to myself. I had walked a mile in her shoes and knew even that length was too much for anyone to have to go through. Eventually I found myself with a form of peace behind this situation. It was no longer me and I did not have to go through the pressure of feeling one way while acting another. Knowing this, I realized I was no longer a hostage to this man nor to his actions. At that moment, I stood up and I moved on with my life. Fear disappeared, nervousness gave way, strength began to flow, and finally I was able to mentally walk away from these memories of that part of my life. For the first time I took a deep breath without worrying if it may be my last by his hands. I remember watching my supervisor one day at my job and for the first time I thought I hope you survive as I did. After that thought, I let go and never looked back. There was more that I wanted in my life right then and there. Holding on to this was no longer an option and I truly acknowledged it as my past. Not long after that decision was made, my ex called again attempting to speak with me. I remember listening to what he had to say, but fear did not rise within me. For the first time a confidence came forth in what I had decided, and I held my grounds with him. After letting him finish speaking, I informed him there were no emotional connection between us as far as I was concerned. I let him know that he was not to call this number again and if he did, I would have a conversation with his fiancé my supervisor. I remember him laughing and stating she would not believe me if I did go to her. Laughing back, I informed him she just may since I was able to tell her what her home number was since he had not been blocking it before calling my house. Silence met my words and the next thing spoken was good-bye before disconnecting. For the first time, I did not have to wrestle with this man and felt drain of strength. For the first time, I opened my mouth and outwitted the enemy in his own actions. Smiling, I sat down on the couch looking at the television while shouting for joy on the inside. Victory was all I could think. Victory was all I could feel. Victory was so little a part of my life that I had to sit in amazement that I had experienced this for the first time. Is it possible that this one moment was reflecting more victories about to take place in my life? Is it possible that by severing the emotions from this experience has now open the door for what I had so long desired? This were the thoughts that began to form in my mind and played with the strings of my heart. My posture had changed, but changed for what had not been seen at that moment. Reality has a way of looking one way to a person, but the truth had yet to be disclosed. Standing, I walked to my bedroom happier than I had been for so long in my life. I felt a flame kindling within me and a hunger to drive forward for everything I wanted. Preparing for bed, I made the decision on when I would begin looking for my new place. The new year was about to roll in and this time it would not leave me out. Not this time. Not ever again.

15

Changes

Life has challenges that come during times we are expecting them and times we are not. Each challenge brings forth a different answer, different actions, and different emotions behind them all. It is easy to respond to challenges, but the answers to them may not always be the effective ones. Sometimes those challenges come back upon a person due to the incorrect answer the first go around. The only thing we know when challenges appear is to provide the best response to them at the time. Even then we are not always sure the answer will be sufficient, but we hope, nevertheless. It was now the year 2010, and as promised I began looking for a new place to live. I would go through town early before work looking for places that had for rent signs outside and putting applications in with different complexes. I knew my friend would be coming home soon, so time was closing in on this. It was February 2010, and my hopes were high that eventually someone would contact me with an opening for me and my family. I was still taking my online courses for my degree with hopes of finding a better position in the field I was majoring in. I was excited and nervous due to the things I had gone through so far. I wanted to have high hopes for the future, but things did not always go the way I wanted or imagined them to. But possibility was still in view for me. Or at least that was where I stood. On night on my day off, I got a phone call from my co-worker during his working hours. I remember thinking he was on one of his breaks and was just calling to speak for a moment. Answering the phone, I could hear the excitement in his voice and asked him what was going on. His next words floored me and caused me to sit up straight for him to repeat what he had just stated. I listened as he asked me do I remember what I had spoken in the break room a few months back about our workplace? Telling him yes, I remember him saying that what I spoke out of my mouth about someone starting a fire there had just taken place. He informed me that all the employees were outside waiting to see if there was any structural damage, but he took that time to call me and share with me what had just happened. Sitting there listening to what he was saying I was completely shocked and numb. His next words were "how did you know this would happen" and my response was I do not know. Asking him was he alright we spoke for a few more minutes. Hanging up the phone, I sat there staring at my bed trying to comprehend the phone call. Something had just happened, and it was confusing to me concerning what it was. How did I know this was going to happen months before it actually took place? This was not the first-time things took place like this, but each time caused me to question what was going on with me. Lying back down preparing to work the next morning, those thoughts dominated my mind until I fell asleep. The next day, I made it to work and observed the outside of it for any damages that took place. Seeing none, I walked on the inside and immediately smelled the scent of smoke heavy within the structure. Going to the back, I overheard other co-workers discussing what had took place and learned there was minimum damage that had been done to the building. It seemed the damage was more focused around merchandise than the physical building itself. Hearing this, I was relieved but still felt questions towards how I had knowledge concerning what would happen before hand. Walking to the front to get my station details, I began wishing my friend were working that day to distract me, but it was his day off this time. Looking around, I saw the supervisor that I attempted to avoid in an means to alleviate issues on those workdays. For some reason she seemed off that morning and it was apparent with her behavior. Shrugging it off, I decided to focus on what I had to do while still thinking over what had just taken place and how I happen to know it. My day was going by quietly and I had no problem with that. Little by little I focused on whether someone would call me with the offer of a new home and the things I needed to do. I remember going on my first break and seeing I had a missed call on my phone with a voicemail message. Not recognizing the number, I listened to the voicemail hoping it was not anything I did not want to deal with. To my surprised, it was one of the landlords I had contacted about an opening they might have responding to let me know there was an availability. At that moment, my nerves became shot as I called the number back to speak with him. Getting him on the phone, he explained to me when the opening would be available for move-in and asked was I still interested. Trying not to scream, I let him know yes, I was and when I should have my deposit and first month rent. Planning to meet the next day after I got off work, I ended the call thanking him repeatedly. I remember sitting there staring at my phone in my hand in total shock. Did this call just happen and was I finally moving forward towards the life I had been dreaming of for the past eight months? Could this really be serious? Every thought imaginable filter through my mind moving each one out of the way to replace it with another. For a moment I forgot where I was and felt tears build into the back of my eyes. Closing my eyes, I took a deep breath before releasing it with every emotion I had carried for two years. Collecting my thoughts, I realized my break was over and I got up to return to my workstation. My motivation levels were higher than ever before, and my joy was starting to bubble over into my actions. I knew my co-workers were wondering what was going on, but I made no attempts to share this with them. I was excited to share with one of them, but it would have to wait until I returned home. Doing my job, I seemed to laugh and talk with each one of the customers that entered my line. My joy felt so overwhelming that I simply had to share with everyone who came through for assistance. Things were starting to go in the direction that I had wanted them to go in when I took this position. True so much had taken place, but the fact that one goal was obtained made all the other things okay. For the moment. I remember hitting the key for a supervisor to come due to my change drawer being low for the day. I only had a couple hours left, but I knew it was not enough for me to finish out the day. I had forgotten about this supervisor was even there and how I was feeling removed any thoughts about what I had observed earlier in the day. Smiling big, I requested more change for my drawer and ignored the look that was thrown my way. Standing waiting for the change to come, I removed my open sign until I was positioned for the next person I would help. My thoughts were reflecting on days to come with moving in, furniture, and other things I would need to complete for this next phase of my life with my family. The fact that an addition may soon be a part of it was the thought that made my smile dance a little bit bigger. So caught up in my thoughts, I did not notice the supervisor returning with my coins request. I remember leaning against my drawer smiling when several rolls of coins hit my station before rolling on to the floor. The impact was so loud that other co-workers and customers turned to look towards the noise. Jumping, I looked up in surprised in an attempt to see what had just took place. Looking at my supervisor, I watched as she snapped her eyes and walked away as if I had offended her in some way. I remember looking down at the coin rolls on the floor of my station and looking back towards where she walked. Anger rose within me and rationality left its place. My only thought was how dare she come and deliberately interrupt my thoughts, my happiness, my dream. Picking up the coins, I placed them inside the cash drawer, but instead of receiving customers I decided to confront her. Walking up the aisle, I heard one of my co-workers call my name and told me not to do it, just let it go. Ignoring them, I considered doing what they said, but they were one of the ones that had laughter at my expense. Pushing their words out of my mind, I walked up to the supervisors' station, located this supervisor, and simply asked her what her issue with me was. Even though I knew the truth, I was simply tired of being treating the way that I was on my job in an attempt to do my job for something unrelated to what I was hired on for. For me, the time had come to either deal with situation physically or verbally. At that point in my life, I just no longer cared which answer came forth. I simply was ready to answer. I could tell that she was shocked I approached her with this question, but I would not back down without an answer. Hearing her response as being nothing, I informed her I knew this not to be true. Finally, she responded that she knew I had been calling her fiancé, my ex, and would like for me to leave them alone. I remember standing there staring at her before laughter fell from my mouth. Seeing that she was offended, I stood there and told her the truth about everything. To solidify my words, I provided her with her own home number to remove any doubts that she may have had from what I was saying. Looking her in the eyes, I told her he is a liar, but it was up to her on what she chooses to believe. Walking away, I was conscious of my back being to her, but I was happy to finally confront this issue. For me, it was over. Things were moving forward and now there was simply nothing back there to discuss.

16

Painful Wait

For everything there is a season for it to take place and purpose behind it. The Bible shares with us that very information, but for those who do not seek the word like that, it would be unbeknownst to them. Every season brings something different, and those seasons are positioned for a reason. The one thing that is an assurance for those times are they are meant to guide one towards a designation no longer within their hands. For every person, the desire to map out their own paths has been a preconceived notion they wanted for themselves. No person expects to go through trials or tribulation, but seasons cannot be defined with those concepts. To build any thing and everything, work must take place to accomplish it. One cannot build an empire without having major construction take place on the designated spot. The same can be stated for a person's life and the construction work they undergo being built. During that season, there comes a waiting period that is a must no matter who or what it surrounds. It is at that time; the season begins to shift from the desires of the flesh into the heart of a servant. I had finally entered a timing where my small family was now living in our own space separate from others. The immense joy from the move was overwhelming and peaceful to my tormented thoughts. The first night in my new home, I laughed in joy that finally I had something of my very own again. My two youngest children were happy to be in this new space, but my eldest showed a desire to be back with my mother. I positioned to her that she could come on the weekend if she so desired in respect to her feelings. I knew my children, especially her, had been through a lot, so this was not an issue for me to give her. I remember her being there with us the first day of the move and could see her attitude changing the more she sat there. Seeing the different things I had already setup for them to have for entertainment was another point for her to stay. Eventually she did come around and my small family was completely together to move forward. Gradually comfort was setting in and we were moving into our own routines of doing things within this household. Time was also near to my friend coming home and excitement levels was beyond measures for me. My mind imagined his reaction to the move, school, employment, and all-around changes implemented while he was gone. The view was perfect in my thoughts to demonstrate what could be with little thoughts to considering anything out of that. Any doubts were quieted, and any nervousness was pushed away. I remained confident that what I imagine would become reality and refused to believe what even my thoughts were trying to state. Finally, the month came for his return and I was overjoyed with the thoughts of our re-connection. Everyday I checked my phone for a missed call or a text at work and at home. But nothing came, no response. One day turned into two and then a week lead into another. The painting in my mind started to look more distorted as each day passed by. After a few weeks of knowing he had returned and not hearing from him, anger started to form. The perfect person I could see myself with started looking more and more like everything else

I had interacted with. Once again depression laughed while calling me stupid to believe I could ever be anything more than an entrée presented to a dinner guest as an afterthought. With little appeal to the palate or any desire for extended sampling after the main course. In my hurt and anger, I verbally abused myself for being the fool I had been for so long to these people I play right into. No one was to blame for my decision but me. So, pointing even at him, was more ignorant to my thinking than just saying it was me. Yes, I was disappointed for ever considering that there was a life in a life that was already built. Allowing the foolish thinking of being loved from "one who understood" was beyond childish in nature, but the illusion of fairy tales was still alive within me. Closing my thoughts to what was now considered a low budget drama film slowly moved into place and the unwillingness of being alone again said hello. During those moments, my attitude and thoughts reflected my emotions with me caring little who knew it. I remember some weeks later being home alone on my day off due to my children going to fair in town. I had just finished cleaning up my home when my phone ranged in the other room. Seeing who the number belonged to, I answered with a happiness to the person calling. We were still very much close, so hearing from her was always interesting to do. Expecting her to say she was coming over was what I thought when I answered the phone, but to my surprised I was informed that this man I was moving to my past was on his way. Staring at my phone, I remember asking her to repeat what she had just stated and listened as she repeated her words. I heard her tell me how the response was to where I was currently located and was told that they were on their way. I walked over to the window to look outside and sure enough the vehicle I remembered was pulling into the neighborhood with a familiar face. I stared in shock and, truthfully, confusion to see what I had waited weeks to see take place. When I wanted it to come it stayed away and now here it was. I informed the caller they were there and let them know I would call them back preparing in my thoughts for what would take place. I was nervous, wary, scared, and a little excited all in one. The one thing I knew was I could not present these things to this man. I could not, was what I thought, but would I be able to do exactly that. I remember hearing a knock on my door and standing there thinking how should I answer? Opening the door, I looked upon this person whom I had wanted to see for almost a year standing before me with that familiar smile. I smiled in return, but my hug was standoffish from his embrace. The hurt was beginning to surface and this was just not something I could fake with him. Inviting him in, I made sure I sat at a distance to avoid any form of physical contact and limited my looks to him. I could feel as well as see him staring at me and now I know it was determining whether my thoughts had shifted away from him. I wish I could say that my stance was stronger than I have written thus far, but flesh was unwilling to let go. True, I fell prey to what my heart desired so strongly once again, but the wait I had endured was preparing me for a visitation I would never forget.

17

Second Invitation

 Anticipation is a powerful emotion that carries more weight than a person could truly understand and realize. The first twinge of its presence can start out in a small capacity, but as time progresses it starts to grow. Along with this emotion, other emotions flood in right along with this one. Before you know it, anticipation turns to connection and that connection evolves into more serious feelings. It is amazing how one emotion can contribute to a hundred more when one is not watching it closely. You find yourself attempting to figure out how did this get from here to here without you realizing what was going on. That is the thing for fleshly desires and its unquenchable thirst for what it wants. Anticipation can cause one to feel as if they have everything they think they could have without one considering they do not. The impact of the truth can be devastating when it comes crashing down on a person, but the aftermath will determine the stance a person chooses to put forth from it. For several weeks, I walked on a portion of cloud nine with the "illusions" of it become complete for me. My new friend was back, and things were going along in a good way in my thinking. I had decided now was the time to really show myself in completeness to this man in hopes that he would see I could fit into his life. Never once did I ponder on whether he would be a fit in mine but fixing myself to look like the image I felt he was seeking. It was late September in 2010 and I had met my time for requesting specific days off from my job. I immediately requested my Sundays since the option was between that day and Wednesday. Excited to be back in church, it felt good going Sunday morning to the household of faith, but there was something seriously off about it. I could not explain it to myself at that time, but it almost felt as if an invisible wall was positioned to block me from coming in. Each Sunday it became more difficult to breath when I entered in and my lungs strained as if I had sat holding my breath during the entire service afterwards. Confused by what was happening while sitting in the building, I never ponder on it once I made it home from church. In October 2010, things were basically the same and my friend had yet made the moves I thought he would eventually do towards me. I became frustrated at one point but was too afraid that if I pushed the subject, I would lose what little I had. I remember one night he called to see was I awake and I let him know I was. Asking if I wanted some company for a little while, I stated that was fine without the normal anticipation that always showed up in my voice when speaking with him. I believe he heard the difference in my tone but chose to not speak upon it. Hanging up the phone, I sat there on my couch and knew something had shifted within me towards this man. Yes, I felt that I still cared deeply for him, but the reality of it was I was tired of hiding my thoughts. I heard the car when it pulled up in front of my building and walked over to unlock the door for him to enter. Sitting back on the couch, I realized I had been here before and knew a moment of reckoning had shown up. Watching him enter my home, I smiled but it was different in its appearance as well as its connection from where it once was. I could tell at that moment, it was not just I who knew things were different, we knew. That night was hard, but I knew it had to be without a doubt. The more I attempted to show my old self that I presented to him that night, the more difficult it was to pretend. I remember walking him to the door as he prepared to leave and him saying goodbye. This goodbye was an agreement that we were moving on without each other. Closing the door to his exit, I leaned against that door in realization that I needed its strength more that it needed me to close it. I cried. I cried until I found the strength to push away from the door and turn away from what I had now come to realize was another fairy tale I had unwittingly played with. Walking to my bedroom, I laid across my bed staring at the shadows interacting on my walls in a playful mannerism. Closing my eyes, I replayed what had just taken place with a small measure of hope that it was just a dream. In that moment it was so quiet and still that a pin drop would have sounded like a bomb. Then suddenly I heard this still deep voice speak and say, "It is time." Sitting up in a hurry, eyes bucked, I looked around my bedroom trying to see how anyone had came in there without me realizing it. Seeing no one, I went to check on my children to see if they were talking, but at that time of night (on a school night) that was not possible. Making sure they were asleep, I walked slowly back to my room and got in the bed still looking around uneasy. I remember lying there afraid and nervous about what had just happened. I do not remember falling asleep, but I do remember dreaming. In this dream, I saw myself riding in a car with two family members. I was sitting in the middle of the backseat sitting forward in between the driver's and passenger's seat. I can remember laughing and talking to them when a large rain drop hit the middle of the windshield in my direct view. I stopped laughing to point out how this raindrop was so huge in its appearance. I leaned over to look out the glass to see a long stretch of a cloud barely visible, but it was there. What caught my attention about this cloud was how it was narrow like the street we were traveling on and that was peculiar. I remember sitting back in my seat, but the curious way that cloud was shaped caused me to look again. This time the cloud was visible and was stretched in the length of the highway we were traveling on. At that point, I looked at my family and prompted them to look at this cloud with excitement. I remember looking back up and the cloud turned from looking like a street to adobe homes that some how I knew were from ancient times. I leaned over more looking at the different structures made from this cloud in amazement and awe. Looking forward through the windshield again, a huge hand made from this cloud appeared with the forefinger pointing directly at me. Suddenly a voice spoke loudly, deep, and clearly stating "I am calling you!" and I woke up. My thoughts were all over the place, but there was no denying what had just happened as well as whose voice this was. I remember thinking how this can be happening to me after what I had just came out of less than 24 hours of what I knew was wrong. Shaking my head, I got up to make sure my children were preparing for school with my mental hands pushing this dream to the back. The problem with this was no amount of pushing would move what I had saw and that voice was repeatedly stating what it has said during my dream. Finally, I knew I needed to speak with someone and at that moment I needed to speak with my mentor so very badly. But that was no longer possible nor an option for me at that point. Thinking on who could I speak with, I saw a face clearly in my thoughts and I immediately called them to share with them that I had saw. I heard their laughter when I began telling them about the words I heard before falling asleep to this dream. I remember feeling confused to why they were laughing until they explained to me their reaction. I heard them say "I knew you had a call on your life but had to wait for God to tell you again." Shocked, I fell backwards in my chair staring through the living room window at nothing. My words at this point were why me, why now, after everything I have done? I walked away from this right at 10 years ago so why bring this back to me now? I heard him sigh and explain to me that "He is God, and He has no respect of a person." Explaining to me where I deemed myself unworthy does not mean God will feel the same way. I listened to him speaking to me and explaining to me the things that I needed to know to the best of his abilities. Getting off the phone a little while later, I sat there still shocked, dazed, confused. My thoughts went back to that time where my mentor was living, and he instructed me to ask God my question then wait for an answer. The answer came back then to my mentor's amusement, but I turned away base off on other's reactions. Lord, why would you still want someone like me and why now were my thoughts. Soon a twinge of excitement began to rise within me and a child like wonder filled my thoughts. Is this possible, can this really be true? Hope once again appeared in my little broken heart and mind, but something else did too.

18

Battlegrounds

Creation is a wondrous yet questionable situation that all have at one point of time thought upon. How everything came to be, why everything came to be, and what the purpose of its formation was for. Even with those questions in the back of our thoughts, we yet still push forward with understanding that those questions potentially will never be answered. So, with that being the case, we must push forward with intentions of living whatever and however it is at this point. With or without the answers we seek. The day I received answers for my life was one I did not consider would appear again from the source that it came from. For me, that time had come and gone surrounded with junk unwelcome in that area. I was still in shock a few weeks later and found myself seeking those within the ministry. At that point in my understanding, women were coming out as preachers, but not in the amount that was noticeable. Or so I assumed. Eventually I was drawn to a couple I had known most of my life or rather they had watched me grow up. I knew that it was stated she was a minister though I had not heard her speak at any time at the church we attended. The first time I went to her, she welcomed me with a smile and a praise to The Lord. Understandably, I could not comprehend this reaction, but it did cause a warm reaction within me. Sitting and talking with her and her husband, I proceeded to explain my visit to their home on that day. Explaining to them about my dreams, visions, and even the messages I had to relay to certain people whose names were given to me. I remember watching their expressions and answering any questions they asked during the conversation to the best of my abilities. I needed to know more about this situation, and these were the people I was sent to for this very thing. Listening intently to what they had to say, I was given instructions to complete and was told to wait. Somehow, I knew this was the right thing to do and so I agreed to what was stated to me. That night I had another dream and was shown myself dressed in a flowing gown with hair down my back. Waking up the next day, I contacted the person I had been going to and was told to contact this leader that they knew. It was explained to me that this leader could help me and tell me what I needed to do as well as how it needed to be done. I remember being nervous and questioned myself on should I really do this or just ignore it for it to go away again? Even though I sat considering this, I knew there was absolutely no way that I could ignore what was happening regardless of what I was thinking. A couple days later, I contacted this leader and spoke with him about what had been happening. He listened without saying a word and asked questions briefly for my answers. After hearing everything I had to say, he advised me to go to my leader and tell him that I had a call on my life I had to answer. He let me know that The Lord had called me once before and now He has brought it back. Hearing the instructions given to me, I agreed that I would do that this very weekend and hung the phone up after we finished speaking. My hands were shaking, my nerves were horrible, and a sense of dread spread through my mind like a tidal wave out of control. There was no doubt that the instructions given to me were correct. They felt right without any hidden agendas or deception surrounding what I was given to do. I went over the scenario continuously until I heard that same voice say, "it is okay." At that point, I let out a deep breath and decided to trust this voice and the words it had just spoken to me. Sunday came before I realized it and I prepared to go complete what I was told I needed to do. I had shared with a few people already what had happened and each time a special joy came behind saying it. Yes, I had begun to experience a happiness behind what had taken place, but there was still an anxiety level that was increasing up until that day. I remember pulling into the church parking lot and sat there looking at the structure as if it were alive waiting on me to enter. I looked around at the cars to see who was there already. I had been instructed to have someone go in with me when I spoke with my leader as a form of witness on my behalf. I had already asked my aunt if she would stand with me and she agreed to do this. Seeing her car, I gather my things and my children for us to go on the inside. I saw that the leader was there already, so I prepared to go in to speak with him. Walking into church, my small family took our seats until the people were dismissed to go to their Sunday school classes. After the dismissal came, I signal to my aunt and we walked together to the leader's office. Knocking and hearing his voice giving permission to enter, I opened the door walking in first and let my aunt close the door behind us. Acknowledging us, I watch the leader look upon us questioningly before explaining to him I needed to speak with him on an important matter. Taking a seat after it was offered, I proceeded to tell him about the words I heard, the dream I had, and what was stated to me. I remember looking him in the eyes the entire time straightforward on the outside, but a complete wreck on the inside. Some how some way, what I was experiencing internally was not expressed in any shape, form, or fashion, outwardly. My posture remained straight, my head remained high, and my gaze never faltered as I spoke. Finishing what I was saying, I asked would he trained me to do what I had been called to do? There was a long pause and I turned to see my aunt standing against the wall by the door as if at any moment she was going to leave.

Looking back at my leader, I watched as he dropped his head, laughed, before speaking. I choose not to disclose that conversation, but I will share that my request was not well received. Sitting there listening to what was being stated to me I neither moved nor dropped my head. After a few minutes of hearing what was being stated, suddenly every word turned into a gurgling noise. I felt this warm feeling, as if a shield had fell surrounding me and blocked what was being said to me about me. I watched my leader's mouth moving but did not understand a word that was being stated. I felt arms wrapped around me with a voice saying, "it is okay" before my leader stopped talking and that shield going away. I did not let on that majority of what had been stated to me I did not hear before standing to leave. I knew I had done what I was instructed to do regardless of what had happened or what had been stated. The point I was proud of myself the most for was I did not ignore what I was told to do and that made me happy. Looking at my aunt, I told her thank you and she asked me what was I going to do? I looked at my aunt and told her I am going to do what God told me to do anyway no matter what. She gave me a surprised look, but eventually smiled while saying okay. Later that day, sitting in regular service, I sat in my normal seat waiting for the moment that the alter call would come. I decided at that moment I would come forth and announce my call to the entire church. When the moment came, I knew that it would not be an easy thing to accomplish no matter my determination to do it. Standing there, with the words in my heart, but a resistance that made it known on that day I would not get what I wanted. No matter how bad I wanted it. After church, I left with the worst feeling I had ever experienced and a decision that it was not over.

19

The Fall

    Intimidation can be a powerful weapon when it is utilized to come against anything a person or a spirit not of God wants to block and stop from coming forth. Through a person, it can be presented in ways surrounding words, gestures, looks, and sounds. Through a spirit, it comes through acts, thoughts, emotions, and situations. Now when you combine those two presences together, every description merges for a violent force that is determined to stop what it does not want to see happen. No matter how it must do it. For a baby walking into a life that is unfamiliar to them, it can be a great tactic that even the strongest person can falter in what they thought they could handle. But this is different. Being in the natural, you only know what is connected to the carnality of life. So, you position what one can consider to be their strength to backup what you can do that way, but even then, that may not be enough. So, if this is the case for the natural aspect of intimidation, the spiritual aspect of this one word can be unbelievable and, yes, frightening when you do not understand. I can say that is the place I found myself facing once again, but this time I was not alone. After that sit down with my leader on that Sunday, I continued to come to church despite what had taken place. I felt determine that I would not be stopped this time but did not understand this was beyond a natural battle. In November 2010, I made my decision to accept my call regardless of it not being received by my covering at that moment. I contacted the leader I was in communication with and stated this to him. He did ask me what happened the Sunday I spoke with my leader and I shared with him what took place.

Even sharing my experience with this warm embrace and shield that deformed the words that were being spoken to me. I asked what I needed to do next to fulfill what I was told to do, and the man of God gave me the right instructions (this I can honestly say). Never once did this man of God encourage me to up and leave but positioned to me the right way of going about everything. Until this day, I am grateful for the right ways being instilled into me from him. Listening carefully, I made a mental note to complete what I was told to do and that night, over the phone, I received the Holy Spirit. That weekend, I prepared to go back to the house of faith that I was still a part of physically yet mentally things had shifted. I could hear and see clearer after receiving my God's spirit to the point it was undeniable. That Sunday, I pulled into the church's parking lot with my family and prepared to go inside with my children. Climbing out of the car, I reached in to grab my bible and purse off the passenger seat beside my daughter. Suddenly I felt this overbearing presence come up behind me causing me to turn from the feeling of a threat. I could see my daughter look at me with a puzzle expression, so I smiled pretending as if nothing had just taken place. Telling my children lets go in, I turned to walk around towards the entrance of the church. I remember glancing around the parking area trying to comprehend what had just happened to me, but no answer fit that reaction. I was walking slowly and cautiously not knowing if anything else would take place. As my small entourage stepped on the sidewalk leading to the front of the church, I held my Bible closer to my side. Right as my feet hit the front of the church, something punched me in my stomach and a sickness slammed into me along with it. I remember reaching out to grab the side of the building while holding my stomach to not heave everything right there on the ground. While leaning over attempting not to be sick, a voice yelled at me not to come in. In that moment, courage was no where to be found and fear yelled at me to agree with this voice. This voice was different. This voice was angry, and this voice was allowing me to feel the hurt it desired to inflict on me. In every way possible. Jerking my hand from the building, I started walking backwards holding my stomach while telling my children come on let us go. I could tell they did not understand what was happening and why I was making them leave when we had just arrived. Explanation was the least thing I was concerned about at that moment. All I knew was the feeling that surrounded me wanted me to understand if I did not leave right then something worst would happen to me. I chose to listen. I remember practically running back to my car and almost leaving my children to keep up with my strives. I was scared. I was afraid. Backing out of the parking lot, I watched the church I attended slowly disappear in my rear view mirror along with that threatening presence. My mind was still trying to understand what had just taken place, but it was just not rational to a mind yet carnal in every way. Later that day, I sat looking at the television, but my mind was still on that morning. Slowly that feeling of self-hate begin to form and I started mentally abusing my very own self. Who was I kidding? Not even this was working out. So maybe what my leader had spoken to me was true and I should just settle on being this way for the rest of my life. That night I accepted my own defeat and turned away from this God I yet did not know once again. The man of God that was assisting me and the others had attempted to contact me after that Sunday. But I never took their calls. I would see the numbers on my phone and ignored them. There was nothing to say. Three weeks had past since that incident outside the church and I made no attempts to go back there. I heeded the warnings that was given to me and made no attempts to do anything different. During that time, the phone calls with my former friend started up again some kind of way. During that first week after that Sunday, he called, and it went from there. I did share with him I had accepted the call into the ministry, and he did sound happy for this decision I had made in my life. I did not share that movement was at a standstill at that moment and chances of anything coming from that decision to grow. I was battling mentally with myself, God, and the devil. In those days, I was completely and utterly powerless to the destruction that wanted to overtake me. In my mind, I was down to the last level I could reach and this time there was no coming up. At least that is what the enemy wanted me to believe, yet where was God.

20

Sin No More

No is a two-letter word that is not always received in an understanding nor welcoming way. When a child hears their parent speak "no" to them towards something they want to do or to say, the tantrum comes with a quickness. Sometimes those tantrums lead to disobedience. Now it is easy to place this description towards a small child or teenager, but we all are children to one Father. It is one thing for a child to disobey their physical parents when they state "no" towards something that child positioned to them. Yet when a higher power says "no", the answer is much more incomprehensible until one finds correction and the ultimate understanding for why it was necessary. It was now December 2010 and the first week of that month started with decisions. I could not ignore the phone calls that were attempting to reach me any longer and was tired of the misery I was living in. I was still very much close to my cousin and leaned heavily on her for my decisions. I can truly say she listened, but never once allowed my self-pity to influence what she had to say. There was no point in going around my situation, so her advice, do what I needed to do. Hearing that, I shut every other thought off in my mind and stated this is right. Either I would remain in this condition for the rest of my life or move forward to see if anything would change. My cousin positioned to me to go and visit the church the man of God I had been receiving advice from was pastoring over. Explaining maybe the atmosphere in that house would help me where I needed it to. Considering it, she let me know she and her family would go with me and I was grateful for the support. That weekend, I prepared to go to church with my cousin to this household of faith that was different from what I knew. Walking in with my family and hers, we found areas in the back to sit together. I remember the Pastor sitting up in the pulpit look towards our direction as we were seated. I watched his facial expression but could not read it. In my mind, I realized this was the man of God that had provided me with instructions on how to move in this call that was unfamiliar to me and my lifestyle. Watching him get up to preach, a pressure fell in the center of my chest that grew in intensity that was almost painful for me. Standing up when he positioned for people to come up for prayer, I glanced at my cousin who nodded in agreement that I should go up. Walking up to the front before these strangers was hard, but I could not stop my legs from moving. Something was up there. Though I could not see it, I felt it standing there waiting. I remember being prayed over and hitting the floor on my knees. This pressure was so strong that all I could manage to do was fold under the weight. I could hear people over me, but even now do not remember what was being said. Suddenly, I heard this voice inside of me and words filling my mouth attempting to burst out while my mind saw every single one of them. The weight of the words became heavy, and I opened my mouth to let them out without thinking over anything I was saying. My only thought was grabbing the words I was seeing and hearing to say exactly what I was shown. I can honestly say I do not remember much after that but going back to my seat. After service, the Pastor spoke with me and let me know he knew immediately who I was when he saw me. I knew this was where I was supposed to be and there were no doubts behind this thought. I setup a time to call him the next day. The time had come to move forward. The following day, I contacted this Pastor and he instructed me on how to move forward in the right way as The Lord desired. Decent and in order. My first step was to obtain a letter from the church through the secretary to exit my old church and enter the new one. My thoughts towards this were doubtful that this would go over well with my current leader, but I agreed to do this much. That first week I made excuses to avoid contacting the secretary, but amazingly the choice was taken out of my hands. I had to run to the grocery store one day that week prior to my children getting out of school to make dinner. I reached over to grab my purse before climbing out of my car. Turning to walk towards the grocery store, I watched as the secretary of my then church exit out. Shocked, I stopped moving and simply stood there staring most likely as if I had saw a ghost. I heard a voice say to go to her right then and before I knew it my feet sprinted towards her before she made it to her car. I greeted her and then presented to her my request for a letter from the church. She asked me what it was for and I explained I am changing my membership while providing to her the name of the new household of faith. Agreeing to complete this for me by Sunday, I thanked her and turned to go complete what I had originally thought I had come to do. Never once did I think I would be faced with my decision, but divine intervention does as He wants. I knew without any doubts my current leader was going to find out about this and prepared my mind for it. Later that evening, a phone call came in and sure enough it was my current leader calling to inquire on my request made earlier that day. Explaining to him this was what God wanted me to do, I listened to what he had to say regarding this. I choose not to share this conversation once again out of respect towards the office. I will say that this time I did not back down, and neither was I torn down. Hanging up the phone, I sat on the edge of my bed smiling while thinking it was almost over. True the structure of buildings was changing, but the structure of the flesh was about to show up. That Sunday, I went to my current church to receive my letter and to stand before this congregation, despite the intimidation, to announce my call. As well as to say goodbye. That day something happened to my spirit, but now it was time for this flesh. Monday of the next week, I went to this new household of faith with my letter and that Sunday I was accepted in. Happiness was not the word I could use to describe how I felt. This was a different walk, but my life had to change. I was still very much involved with this man who still only offered me the alternative lifestyle. With everything that was taking place, I was sure that this could go somewhere. Things had shifted in his life, but the path seemed to have included more people outside of me. A day finally came for a truth that neither I expected and, honestly, he did not as well. I remember him calling and asking was I home before coming over that day. I found it strange that he was coming like this on his day off, but excitement filtered in that this was the moment I had waited for. Upon his arrival, it felt like for a brief second a family completed finally. He interacted with my children and my heart was overjoyed to see imagination reflect as reality. In my thinking. My children prepared for bed and I sat talking with this man amazed that he was still here. I could hear this voice saying, "let him leave", but I refused to let this moment go. Why would I tell the person I saw myself with to leave when I had prayed for so long for one to be on the opposite side of the door with me? Those words hammered into my thoughts until I put them on mute. Every moment I felt torn, and every second became uncomfortable. The bliss I thought I would continue to have became more and more sour to my taste. My flesh was a trap and had come into agreement with the adversary. It did not want this lifestyle I had taken on and with one final assault it rebelled against my decision to shut it down. The fall was hard and bitter to the very core. When I thought I could not go any lower, I found there was a level of lowness that is further down to drop. I heard my flesh react in a hideous joy and the enemy wrapped up in complete glee. My head lowered, and tears falling from my eyes, I said from the inner most part of my heart "Lord, forgive me." Before my heart could finish asking what was within it, a presence filled my room that was so powerful, I knew at that moment my soul could have been crushed under the magnitude of it. Looking down, too afraid to look up, I heard this voice like a great and powerful horn say, "You are forgiven. Now sin no more." Hearing this, I cried and said "yes, sir" before the presence was lifted from my room. Still afraid to look up, I slowly lifted my head scanning my bedroom. What had just happened was real and I knew mistakes like this was no longer an option to make from that day forward. On that night, I made the decision to do what I had been chosen to do for The Lord and no one else. I gave my God my word I would not compromise who He is and who I am for Him. That decision has not changed and, to God be the glory, it never will. Fate may have had its influence, but destiny was never in its hands. God gave me my story for His ultimate glory in my life. God bless.

21

Epilogue

Epilogue
This chapter is dedicated to all those who have had an impact on my life and the journey I am now fulfilling through God's call. Thank you to every one of you for the inspiration, the teaching, the prayers, the talks, and the instructions you gave unto me. Though I have lost some before and after the journey, God's faithfulness always replaced. I honor each one of you and I will forever be grateful to what you have poured into my life. I am going to run on and see what the end looks like. God bless you.

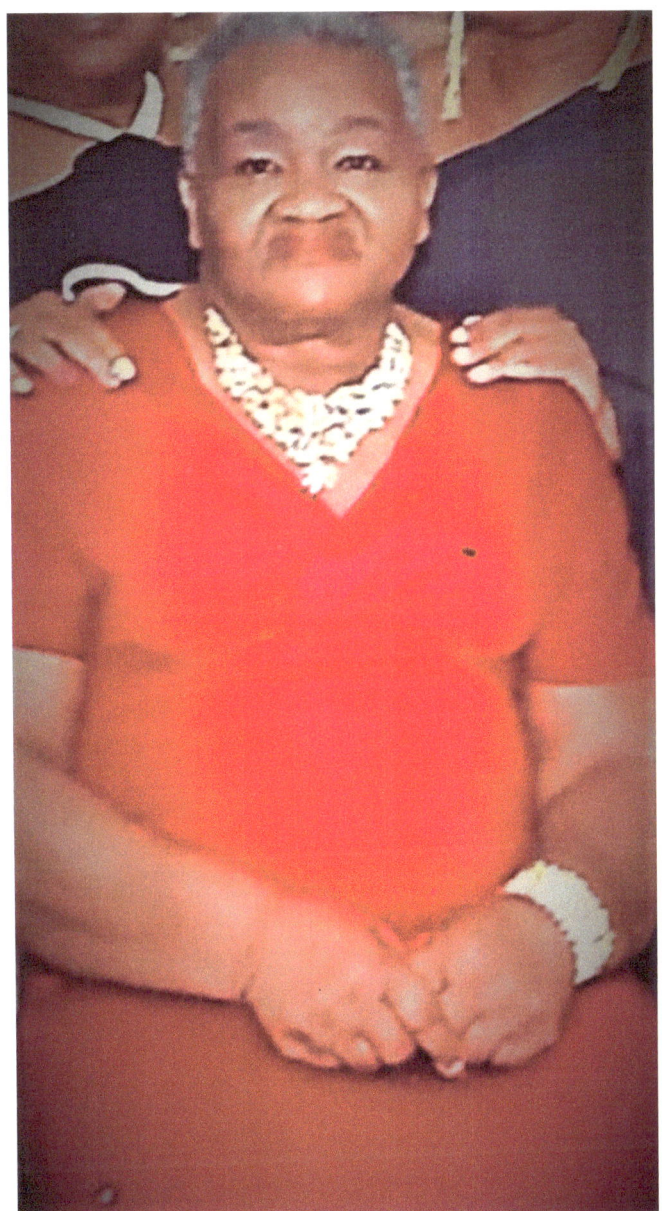

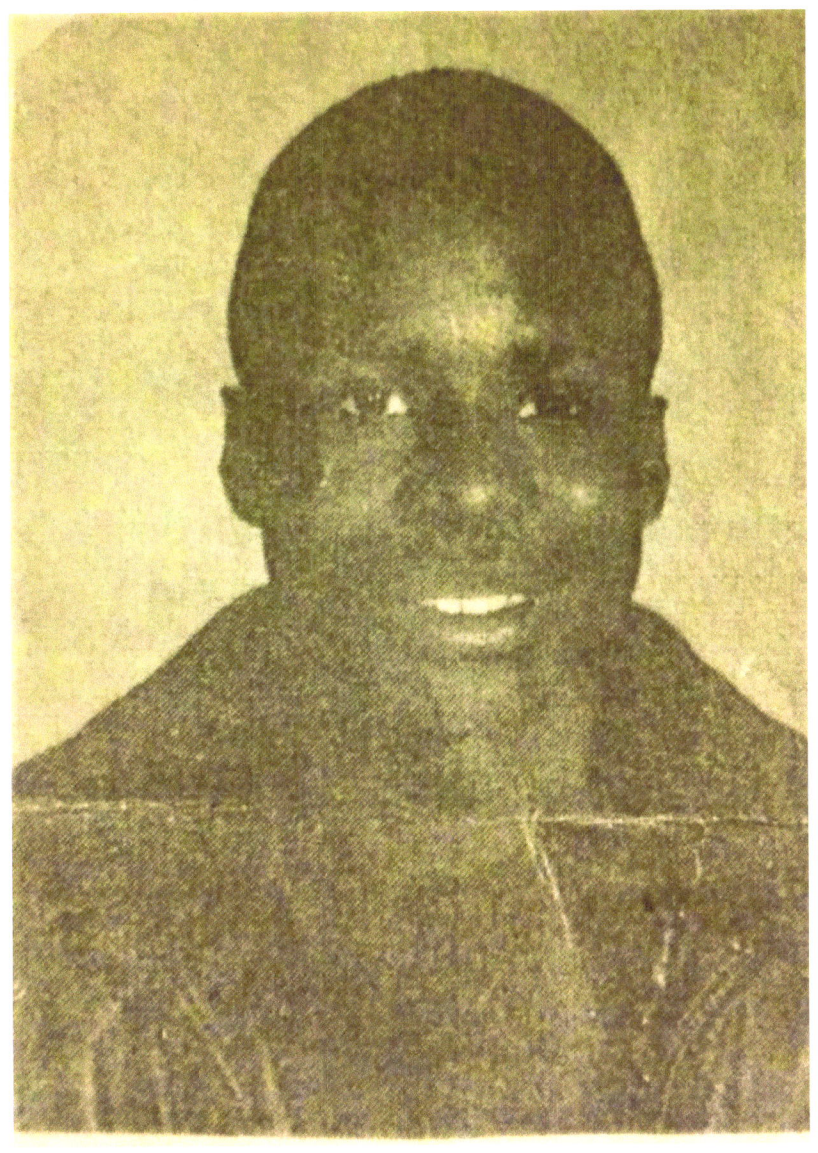

www.ingramcontent.com/pod-product-compliance
Lightning Source LLC
Chambersburg PA
CBHW040202100526
44592CB00001B/6